Contents

chapter 1: beginnings

XTREME SPORTS

ROCK CLIMBING

by Kate Cooper

ticktock

The author

Dr. Kate Cooper was born in Colne, Lancashire in 1961. She studied mathematics and wrote her doctoral thesis on computability theory. Her first taste of rock climbing was in 1988 at Yorkshire's famous gritstone outcrop, Almscliff. In 1999 she began climbing regularly, first indoors at the Leeds Wall, then on the gritstone and limestone crags of Yorkshire and Derbyshire. When she can, she travels further afield to climb in Cumbria, Wales, Dartmoor and Spain. Her favourite rock type is rhyolite. She has a son and a daughter, both of whom climb.

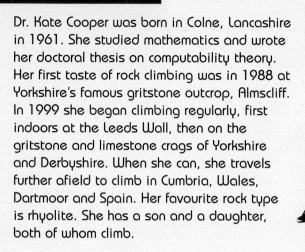

Copyright © ticktock Entertainment Ltd 2008

First published in Great Britain in 2008 by ticktock Media Ltd,
2 Orchard Business Centre, North Farm Road, Tunbridge Wells, Kent, TN2 3XF

ticktock project editor: Julia Adams
ticktock project designer: Sara Greasley
ticktock picture researcher: Lizzie Knowles
editor: Ben Hubbard

With thanks to: Nick Smith, Keith Sharples, John Cleare, Trudi Webb, Diana LeCore, Marc Adams, Anna Brett

The author wishes to thank Mick Ryan, Toby Foord-Kelcey, Stuart Anderson and the many helpful posters of the UKClimbing.com discussion forums for their invaluable feedback and advice, and also Evan and Natasha, for their support and patience.

References
1. Spread on the North Face of the Eiger uses information fromThe White Spider, by Heinrich Harrer.
2. Spread on Todd Skinner and The Nameless Tower uses information from Todd Skinner's website, Beyond The Summit:
http://www.beyondthesummit.com/exp_summ.html
3. Spread on Lynn Hill, Warren Harding and The Nose uses information from Supertopo, at supertopo.com
http://www.supertopo.com/

ISBN 978 1 84696 524 1 pbk

Printed in China

Picture credits (t=top; b=bottom; c=centre; l=left; r=right):
4Corners images/ SIME/Giovanni Simeone: 10/11t. Alamy/ David Hosking: 9b. Aurora Images: 8 (Jose Azel), 33cl (Corey Rich). Josune Bereziartu: 14/15. Dave Bennet: 16/17t. Neil Bentley Collection: 37b. Boreal: 17cr. Simon Carter/ Onsight Photography: 61b. John Cleare: 4/5, 13t, 57b, 60t, 61t. Katherine Cooper: 2. Steve Crowe: 49cl. Cubby Images: 48, 49t. Chris Dainton: 52/53. Ged Desforges: 43t. Greg Epperson: 57t. The Fell and Rock Climbing Club: 11cr, 12 inset. Graeme Gatherer: 19cl. Jack Geldard: 19b. Getty images: 18, 40/41t (Mike Powell), 47br (AFP), 51t (AFP). John Gill: 51b. Tim Glasby: 19t. Matt Hartgrove: 21t. Andrew Huddart: 43b. iStock: 1. Rob Lillywhite: 21cl. Josh Lowell: 44/45 (from the movie KING LINES, www.bigUPproductions.com) 24/25 (from the movie DOSAGE VOL IV, www.bigUPproductions.com). Dave MacLeod: 46b. Chris McNamara: 56. Alex Messenger: 47bl. Bobby Model /M-11 Images: 55t, 55b. Gwen Moffat/ S.R.G Bray: 13b. Frédéric Moix: 49cr. National Geographic: 6t (Getty Images), 54. Chris Noble: 50b. Peter O'Donovan: 38/39. PA Photos/ AP: 59b. Rich Potter: 17bl, 27bl. Galen Rowell / Corbis: 33t. Keith Sharples: 7c, 20, 23b, 32. Shutterstock: 3, 9t, 10b, 11bl, 19cr, 42, 46/47t, 58. Nick Smith: 22, 23t, 26, 27t, 28 all, 29all, 30, 31t, 31b, 34, 35t, 36. Gordon Stainforth: 35b. Superstock/ Age fotostock: 37t. PRESTON UTLEY/AP/PA Photos: 50t. Stewart Watson: 7t. Donald Willey: 12. Jörg Zeidelhack: 41t.

Every effort has been made to trace copyright holders, and we apologise in advance for any omissions. We would be pleased to insert the appropriate acknowledgments in any subsequent edition of this publication.

Iconic British climber Joe Brown scaling Spiders Web on Gogarth North Stack, UK (1970).

Rock climbing is more than a sport – it's a passion and a way of life. It's about movement, strength and balance. It's also about learning how to use your body in harmony with the rock, and keeping a cool head when you're afraid.

All sorts of people climb. Men and women can excel equally. Height doesn't matter either – there are top climbers who are only five feet tall, and others well over six feet.

ROCK CLIMBING

Devils Tower, Wyoming, USA –
a popular climbing destination

Sabine Bacher at the climbing World
Championships in Bulgaria, 2007

Ben Moon's attempt to climb Big Bang,
The Great Orme, UK

People climb all over the world, on rock
that ranges from small boulders to great
mountains with rock faces over 1,000
metres high.

Climbing is a dangerous
activity – you can do
everything right and still
end up dead. This book
tells you a bit about
climbing and climbers,
but it does not tell you
how to climb. If you
want to climb, check
out your nearest
climbing-wall gym.
At a good wall, expert
instructors can teach
you the skills you
need to climb as
safely as possible.

Nowadays, people climb for joy. But long ago people climbed just to survive. In a remote desert in Mali, Africa, a sandstone cliff juts hundreds of metres into the blue sky. Caves can be seen dotted over the rock face – thousands of years ago the Tellem people lived in these caves.

Cave

A Dogon man climbs the cliffs

Caves

No-one knows why the Tellem people chose to live so high up, but it may have been to avoid slave traders. These days, the Dogon people live by the foot of cliffs. They climb them, searching the caves for valuable Tellem artifacts. Dogon myths say that the Tellem were witches, who could fly to their caves.

The White House Ruins

White House

The White House Ruins, part of the Canyon de Chelly National Monument in Arizona, USA, is an 800-year-old stone village built by the Anasazi people. Their homes could often only be reached by climbing or using ropes.

St. Kilda

People inhabited the rocky islands of St. Kilda, Outer Hebrides, Scotland, until the 1930s. The journey to the mainland was treacherous and impossible to make in the winter. The isolated islanders ate seabirds, which lived in the cliffs. They had to scale the cliff faces to catch the birds and gather their eggs. They ate seabird flesh, seabird eggs and even wore shoes made of seabird skins. They sometimes ate fulmar – a type of seabird – three times a day.

The rugged St. Kilda cliffs

The earliest climbers climbed to collect food or escape danger. In later centuries, powerful rulers would order their subjects to climb mountains to celebrate victory, pay religious tribute, or even just to show off.

Mont Aiguille is a gigantic rock in France, with vertical walls over 300 metres high. In the Middle Ages it seemed impossible that anyone could ever reach the top, so it was known as the "Inaccessible Mountain".

The sure-footed chamois

In 1492, Charles VIII, King of France, commanded his soldier Antoine de Ville to climb the "Inaccessible Mountain". Antoine and a dozen men used ladders and grappling hooks to attempt the climb. It took several days, and Antoine called the ascent "the most horrible and frightful passage", but they did it. At the top they discovered a beautiful meadow grazed by a herd of chamois, a type of goat.

Mont Aiguille – there are no easy ways to the top

In the 18th century people began to climb mountains purely for adventure. In 1786, Italians Jacques Balmat and Michel Paccard reached the summit of Mont Blanc, the highest mountain in western Europe. This was the start of modern mountaineering.

Ladies and gentleman on a glacier, Switzerland, 1895

Mont Blanc is 4,807 metres high

In the mid-19th century, mountain climbing became increasingly popular, with many Alpine peaks being climbed for the first time.

At first, rock climbing was simply a way of getting to the top of a mountain peak – no-one cared much what techniques were used. But gradually that attitude changed. In the 1880s, English athlete Walter Haskett Smith started scrambling in the Lake District.

Walter Haskett Smith

Walter soon moved on to soloing rock climbs. He relied on his own strength and skill rather than using ladders, ropes and hammering spikes into the rock. His goal wasn't primarily to reach the top – there was usually an easier way up – he climbed purely for pleasure. In 1886 he made the first ascent of Napes Needle. This daring exploit captured the imagination of the British nation, and the new sport of rock climbing was born.

Napes Needle in the English Lake District

Walter Haskett Smith

Soloing Climbing on your own without a rope to protect you.

Scrambling A freestyle mix of climbing and walking.

Joe Brown

One of the UK's most respected climbers and mountaineers, Joe Brown was dubbed 'The Human Fly' because of his extraordinary ability to cling to steep rock. "For me, the enjoyable part of climbing lies in the adventure," Joe says.

Joe Brown in the Wen Zawn area of Craig Gogarth, Anglesey, UK (ca.1974)

Gwen Moffat

Born in 1924, Gwen Moffat was as tough as any of the men she climbed with. She lived rough, sleeping under hedges, and later hitch hiked to the Alps to become the first British female mountaineering guide.

Gwen Moffat climbing Superdirect, Wales, UK (1956)

chapter 2: basics

Spanish Josune Bereziartu, the world's top female sport climber (pictured here), said of the day she climbed the ultra-hard route, Bain de Sang (Saint Loupin, Switzerland) in 2002: "While I was warming-up I felt those feelings deep inside you that make you realise that something is special."

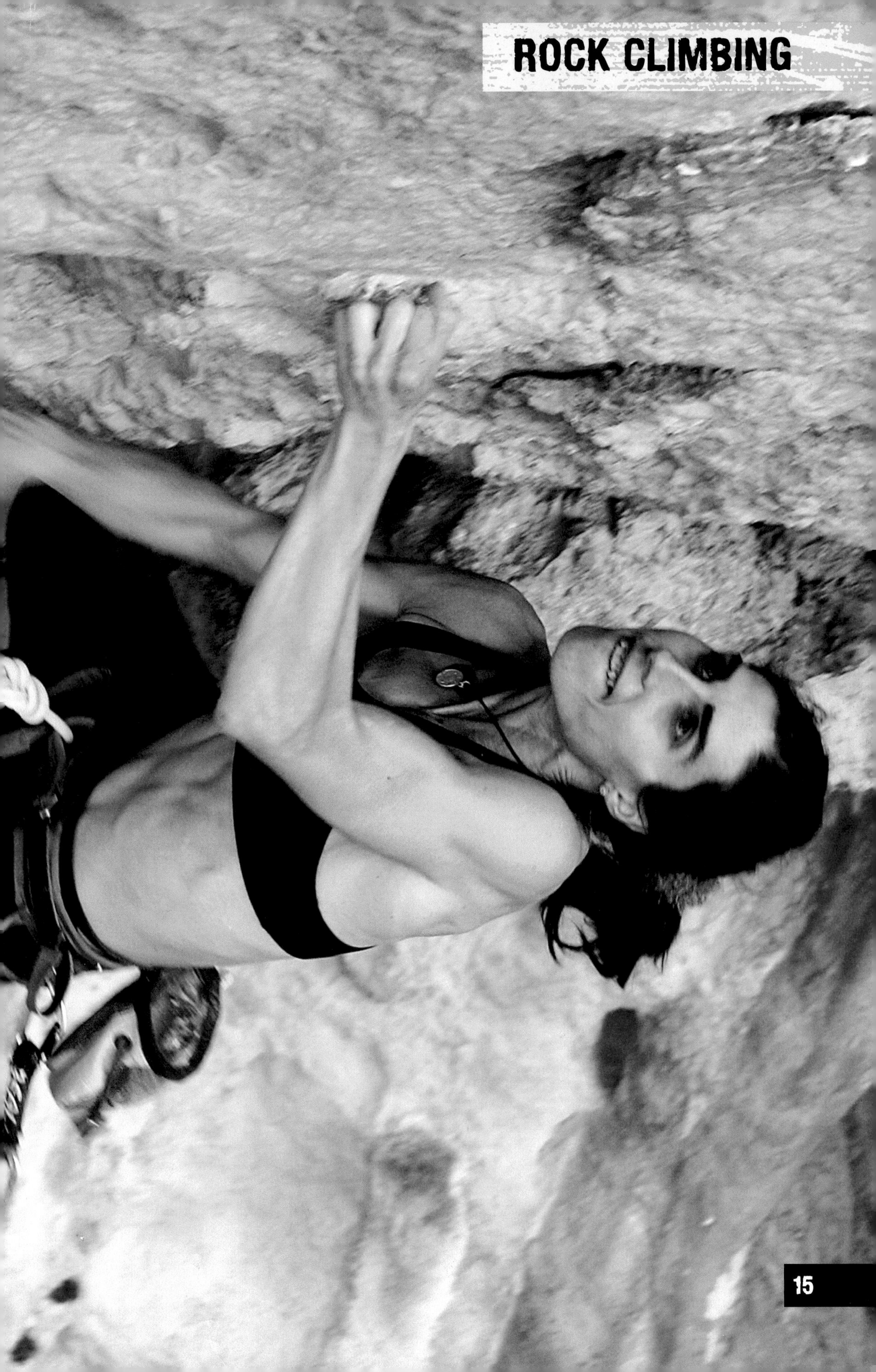

Climbing boots – or 'stickies' – are the most basic piece of climbing gear. Modern climbing shoes are designed to fit very tightly, giving the climber's feet a tough second skin of rubber. The rubber is special – it moulds to the rock surface, helping the climber grip tiny footholds.

Rubber strap: helps shoe keep its claw-like shape

Sole: with very sticky rubber

There are different styles of climbing boots for different sorts of climbing: from high-tech slippers used by elite boulderers, to more comfortable shoes suitable for wearing all day on long climbs.

Highly technical shoes squash the climber's toes so that they are curled. That can be very uncomfortable, so they are only worn during the actual climb. Climbers wear ordinary sports shoes to walk to the crag, and often take their shoes off between routes.

Velcro straps: quick to put on and take off

Loop at the heel: the loop helps the climber pull on the very tight boots.

Ridged heel: for increased grip

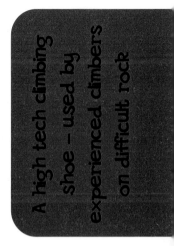

A high tech climbing shoe – used by experienced climbers on difficult rock

Curved rand: curves the foot, helping the climber pull with their feet

This is a popular all-round shoe. Although it is still snug fitting it is relatively comfortable to wear, and is suitable for most ordinary climbers.

Big wall shoe

An all-purpose climbing boot

Big wall shoes are boots used for climbing mountainous rock routes which may take several days to complete. They are a cross between a climbing boot and a hiking boot.

A climber's clothing has to allow free body movement, keep the climber warm and have layers that are easily shed, as climbing heats you up.

One of the world's top speed climbers, Indonesian Muslim climber, Etti Hendrawati, climbs in her hijab and long trousers out of respect for her faith

Trousers

Climbing trousers should be non-restrictive, giving flexibility and a clear view of the feet. They are often made from tough, light, quick-drying, abrasion-resistant fabric.

Duvet jackets

Climbers often get cold when they're at the bottom of the route holding their climbing partner's rope. A duvet jacket is full of goose down, so it is lightweight and warm.

Chalk

The bag a climber wears around their waist contains a white powder: magnesium carbonate. This is a type of chalk. It helps climbers grip by absorbing sweat from their hands.

Helmet

Not all climbers choose to wear helmets, but it is definitely a must for beginners. A helmet protects the climber's head in case they fall or are hit by falling rocks.

Pete Robbins heel
hooks on Cromlech
Boulder, Wales, UK

Climbers love the feel and flow of climbing. They have lots of different moves they use to get up the rock. They might be stretching high, up on tiptoes for one move; then crouched with their feet together, knees apart like a frog for the next.

One such climbing move is called a heel hook, which involves getting one leg up high, so that you can pull with your heel almost as though it's an extra hand. A heel hook helps to shift the weight from your arms to your raised leg on steep ground.

This move is called an Egyptian, after side-on figures from ancient Egyptian wall paintings

Moving terms

• A dyno is a move used when you can't reach the hold you want by stretching, so you jump to it.

• Jamming means shoving a bit of your body in a crack in such a way that it'll take your weight with very little muscular effort. There are foot jams, fist jams and hand jams. Which part of your body you jam depends both on the route and what size you are.

• Smearing is moving up by placing the sole of the front part of your foot flat against the rock.

Here, a climber laybacks. Laybacking is a move where you stay in balance by pulling with your arms and pushing with your legs. It feels great, but can be strenuous as it puts a lot of weight on your arms.

There are dozens of different types of rock, each with its own special characteristics. A climber will adjust their climbing style and technique to the sort of rock they are climbing.

Climbing on gritstone at Stanage Edge, Peak District, UK

Gritstone

Peak gritstone was formed from sand laid down at the bottom of lakes and rivers around 300 million years ago, when sharks swam in the seas but dinosaurs had not yet evolved. Gritstone gives good friction for the climber's feet, but has typically rounded handholds, which climbers call slopers.

Limestone

Limestone is made from the bones and shells of tiny creatures that lived in shallow seas millions of years ago. It often gives good handholds. On some limestone routes you can even see fossils in the rock.

Tufa

Tufa is deposits of calcium carbonate, the same mineral that forms stalactites and stalagmites in caves.
It can give big jugs – jutting holds that are easy to pull up on – making it possible to climb on very steep rock.

Climbing grades Climbing routes are graded according to how hard they are to climb. They are graded by the first person to ascend them, and then may be re-graded if subsequent climbers disagree. Different countries use different grading systems, and there are different systems for different sorts of climbing. The one thing they all have in common is, the bigger the number, the harder the route. So, for example, an E5 is harder than an E4. The E stands for 'extreme' and is used to grade trad routes. So far, the hardest route is graded at E11 (Rhapsody, Dumbarton Rocks, Glasgow, UK).

chapter 3: roped climbing

American Lisa Rands was the first woman to climb E8 grade routes in the Peak District, UK, where a fall could mean hitting the ground from over 15 metres.

When climbers use ropes they climb in pairs. Firstly, the climber is tied to one end of the rope. Then their partner, called the belayer, is linked to the rope via a special rope-brake called a belay device.

Belayer and their climbing partner

Belay

The belay device lets the belayer slide rope out as the climber goes higher. When used correctly, the belayer will stop the rope slipping through if the climber falls off. The belayer holds the rope firmly all the time – called belaying. It is a vital job that takes skill and experience to do well.

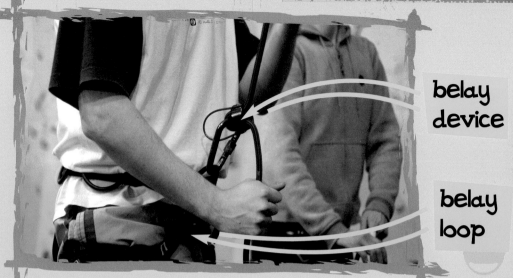

belay
device

belay
loop

A belay device and belay loop

Belay device

This is a popular type of belay device. When the belayer holds the rope properly, the device creates a zigzag in the rope which stops the rope slipping through it. A belayer literally holds the life of their partner in their hands.

A climber
wearing a harness

Harness

A climbing harness enables the climber and belayer to attach themselves to the rope. The webbing waistband doubles back through the metal buckle.

Belay loop – a strong loop at the front for attaching the rope and belay device when belaying (see above).

Gear loops – small plastic loops for hanging climbing gear on when it isn't being used.

Leg loops – strong bands which support the legs so that when the climber falls their weight isn't only on their waist.

A climber places
a wire in a crack

To protect themselves when climbing on natural rock, a climber uses special chunks of metal and strong straps collectively known as gear to temporarily link their rope to the rock. Climbing this way is called trad climbing.

Cam

A cam is a mechanical device that can be narrowed by pulling a lever. Then it can be slotted into a crack. When the lever is released, the cam automatically opens wider and wedges itself in the crack.

Wires

Wires are small, wedge-shaped chunks of lightweight metal, threaded on strong stiff wire. Some chunks are tiny, others much bigger. They slot into different sized cracks.

Hex

A hex works much like a wire but is bigger, so it slots into bigger cracks. It gets its name from its six-sided, hexagonal shape. Because hexes are hollow they are quite light.

Slings

Slings are straps of woven fabric tape formed into a loop. They are much stronger than ordinary fabric, and very secure when threaded around an immovable rock.

Karabiners and quickdraws

A karabiner is a metal oval with a hinged opening section. Some screw shut, others snap shut. A quickdraw is made from two karabiners joined by strong fabric-tape. Quickdraws link the gear to the rope.

When a climber gets ready to climb, they fasten their harness, attach their gear, then tie the rope to their harness using special knots.

Leader placing first piece of gear

Leading

Once the belayer is ready, the leader begins to climb – they are leading the route. The belayer is there to try and stop the leader hitting the ground if they fall, by holding the rope which the climber will attach to the rock as they climb. At first, if the leader falls off there is nothing to stop them hitting the ground.

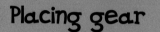

Climber with two pieces placed

Placing gear

As soon as they can, the leader places gear – often in a crack – and attaches the rope to it using a quickdraw. If they have placed the gear well it will stay snugly in the rock if they fall off. As long as they are not too high above it, the belayer can stop them hitting the ground if they fall. The higher the leader is, above their last bit of gear, the bigger a fall will be.

For example, if a leader falls off when two metres above their last gear, they will fall well over four metres. This is twice the distance they were above the gear, plus however much slack rope there is between the leader and the belayer. So for the leader to be safe, they need to place gear well, and often, and have a belayer who manages the rope carefully.

Seconding

When the leader reaches the top, they fasten themselves securely to the rock. Their partner stops belaying and ties onto the other end of the rope. The leader pulls up any slack rope. Then it's the leader's turn to belay their partner, who climbs up, removing all the gear as they go. This is seconding.

Second going up, removing gear

Steve McClure does a bat hang
on his new route, Overshadow, on
Malham Cove, Yorkshire Dales, UK

Not all routes have good places for gear, instead they may have bolts
permanently set in the rock. The climber carries quickdraws and clips
them to the bolts as they reach them. This is called sport climbing.

In the UK, bolts are only placed on rock that cannot be climbed in trad style,
as climbers like to change the rock face as little as possible. Some rock is
never bolted, however few places there are for gear. This makes the route
more dangerous, which is part of the challenge.

Warren Harding climbing on the Half Dome, Yosemite Valley, USA

Free climbing and aid climbing

Trad climbing and sport climbing are different sorts of free climbing. In free climbing, the climber uses their rope and gear to protect themselves in case they fall. But a climber who is aid climbing, puts sturdy metal objects into the rock and uses them for hand or foot holds. For example, when Warren Harding climbed The Nose on El Capitan (Yosemite Valley, USA) he hammered cooking stove legs into one wide crack to give himself something secure to pull up on!

Beth Rodden climbing on a sport route

Many climbers like to push themselves to their limits on sport routes because they don't have to worry about badly placed gear ripping out if they fall.

A roped climber falls through the air

When a climber falls, their life depends on their gear and their belayer. Climbers at the cutting edge of the sport climb the hardest routes and can fall off a lot.

Falling

When a climber falls off, the rope between them and the belayer pulls tight very suddenly. The bigger the fall, and the heavier the climber, the stronger the pull on the belayer. Big falls can sometimes pull a light belayer up in the air. This can be avoided by using gear to fasten the belayer to the ground.

34

A climber falls, but is saved from injury by their rope

Rope

Modern climbing rope is very strong. It is also dynamic – as the falling climber's weight pulls the rope, it stretches. This brings the climber to a relatively gentle halt. Non-stretching, or static rope, cannot be used for climbing. Even quite a short fall on static rope can kill the climber.

Before harnesses were invented climbers wore a hemp waistband

Hemp Before World War II, climbers used hemp rope. They looped the rope over spikes of rock as they climbed, hoping that it would save them if they slipped. But hemp isn't strong – taking a big fall was unthinkable. It was also hard to undo when it got frozen. Climber Keith Sutcliffe says "I remember on winter days not being able to undo the fisherman's knot in the hemp waistline, and going home, stripping off and getting in the bath with waistline on to undo it."

If a rock face is higher than the length of the rope, the climber cannot get to the top in one go. In this case, they stop at a ledge, attach themselves securely as if they were at the top, and belay the second climber up.

Pitch

On these very high rock faces, the climber often has to repeat the process; of stopping at a ledge and belaying the second all the way to the top. Each section of the route is called a pitch.

Some routes don't have enough ledges to do this. In this case, the lead climber has to attach themselves to the rock and hang from it while they belay their second up to join them. This is called a hanging belay.

Climbers on a multi-pitch trad route

Trad or sport

Multi-pitch routes can be trad, with the climbers placing and removing protection as they go; or sport, with bolts in place for protection.

Two climbers on a long
multi-pitch sport route

Portaledges

Some rock faces are too high to be climbed in one day. The climbers have to haul up bags containing the food, drink and fuel they need. They sleep on artificial ledges called portaledges. The haul-bags and portaledge must be secured to the rock so that they can't fall down. A portaledge dangles on a single loop, which has to be extremely strong.

Climbers resting on a portaledge

chapter 4:
climbing without a rope

Climber and mountaineer Andy Cave, bouldering in the Wool Packs, Kinder Scout, UK. Andy remembers his first climb, as a teenager: "I rushed back to the base of the cliff, like a small child having just tasted sugar for the first time."

Climbing doesn't have to be about getting up high. Bouldering is unroped climbing on low rock. Bouldering routes are called problems.

Boulderers often use portable bouldering mats or pads. They are folding, portable mattresses made of special foam that is good at absorbing impacts. The climber may repeatedly jump or fall off onto the mat as they struggle with a hard move. Boulderers often like to climb in groups, taking it in turns to try challenging problems in a spirit of friendly competition and encouragement.

Dai Koyamada on The Wheel of Life, Hollow Mountain Cave, Australia — one of the world's hardest bouldering problems

Born in 1976, Dai Koyamada grew up in the countryside of Western Japan. He made his own climbing wall inside his garage after seeing a photo of an alpine climber. After climbing The Wheel of Life (Australia), he said: "Under the clear blue sky, the cool dry air eases my burning muscles; the feeling of joy beyond description."

Those watching may stand ready to help protect the boulderer in the event of a fall. This is called spotting. The spotter's job is to make sure the climber's head and spine don't hit the ground. They push the falling climber in the direction of the bouldering pad to try to give them a safe landing. Even short falls can be dangerous, and whilst mats and spotters help prevent injury, they do not eliminate the risk.

Soloing is climbing alone, usually without a rope. This is the most risky form of climbing – the climber is high enough for a fall to kill, or seriously injure them.

Risks of soloing

Even when the climber is on a route they would normally find easy, events outside their control may make the ascent more dangerous:

• Dry weather might change to rain – wet rock is often slippery.

• A handhold might pull off – quite common on some rock types.

• They might be hit by rockfall.

Despite these risks, many climbers enjoy soloing and the feeling of freedom and lightness it gives them.

The south face of the Marmolada, the highest peak in the Dolomites in the Alps

The Fish

On 29th April 2007, Hansjörg Auer stunned the climbing world when he soloed a route known as The Fish, on the south face of the Marmolada in Italy. Amazingly, Hansjörg completed around 915 metres of exceptionally hard climbing in under three hours.

The Fish, Dolomites, Italy

Deep water

Deep-water soloing is soloing above water that is deep enough to break the climber's fall. However, like everything else about climbing, deep-water soloing involves many complex skills that have to be learnt. It should be left to the experts.

Chris Sharma said about deep-water soloing: "That's how I want climbing to be for me, just free."

A climber falls off a deep-water solo into the sea

chapter 5: rockstars

American climber Chris Sharma was the first to climb a sport route with an agreed grade of 5.15a – Realization, Ceuse, France – and the only climber so far to have climbed multiple sport routes of that grade.

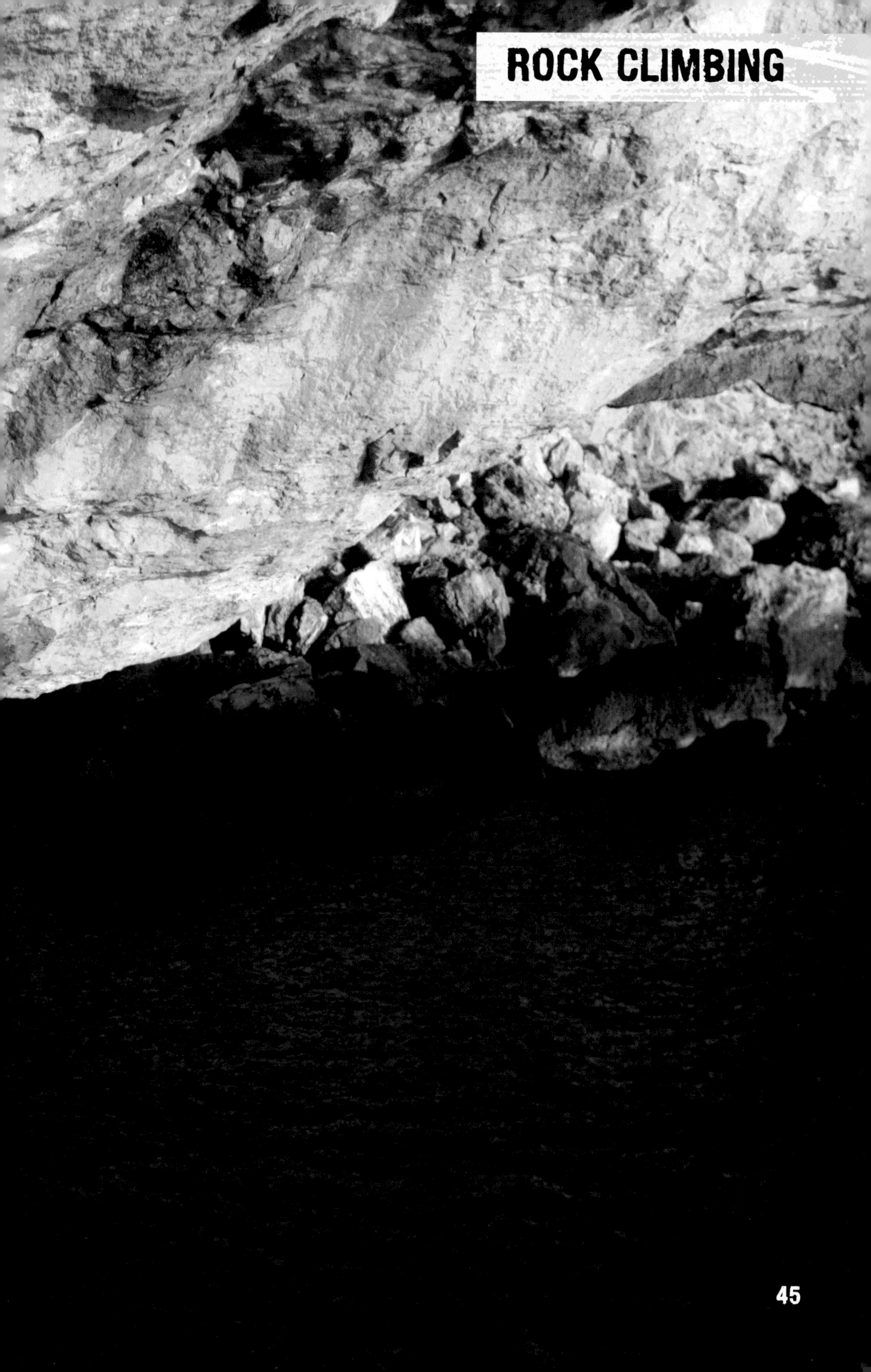

Top climbers have to work extremely hard to climb at their peak. They pay attention to their diet and train their bodies to be as strong as possible. An elite climber will often use a climbing wall to maximise their fitness.

Climbing walls often host competitions. The walls themselves are designed to mimic natural rock or have bolt-on and screw-on holds. Climbers compete to see who can climb the hardest routes or problems. There are specific competitions for children, with age banded categories. There are also speed-climbing competitions in which climbers try to climb a set route in the fastest possible time.

Climbers like Dave Macleod use fingerboards to improve their upper body strength

Ramón Julián Puigblanque from Spain won the 2007 Rock Master competition in Arco (Trentino, Lake Garda, Italy). Rock Master is the world's longest-running climbing competition. Ramón is a top sport climber on natural rock, as well as excelling at competition climbing.

French climber Sandrine Levet winning the 2006 Rock Master competition in Arco, Italy

Ramón Julián Puigblanque, Rock Master competition 2007

For most climbers, rock climbing is about being out on natural rock. Because of this, the most famous climbers are not necessarily competition winners, but those who climb the hardest routes. Being the first ascentionist of a hard rock route takes incredible levels of commitment and courage.

Scottish climber Dave MacLeod, climbing on Rhapsody, grade E11

ROCK CLIMBING

Dave MacLeod: "The primary thing that makes me want to climb all the time and do hard routes is to exercise my imagination."

In 2006, Dave Macleod climbed the world's hardest trad route, Rhapsody, at Dumbarton Rock in Scotland. Climbing Rhapsody, he endured many falls of 21 metres onto a tiny wire. Sometimes it snapped, but he was never seriously injured enough to stop him returning to the route. Eventually he knew the rock so well that he practiced the sequences of moves in his head.

British Lakeland climber Dave Birkett made the hardest trad onsight ascent in the world by climbing Fear of Failure (E8 6c) at Dove Crag, Lake District, UK

Onsight literally climbing a route on sight – without practising on it beforehand or falling off.

Most amazing young climber?

Bouldering is measured in V grades. The easiest problems are V0, then V1, V2 and so on. When she was only 8, American Cicada Jenerik climbed a V7 boulder problem. When she was 10, she climbed a V10. And when she was 11, she climbed a V11. No one else has ever bouldered their age.

Fastest climber?

Dan Osman was one of the fastest climbers there has ever been. He soloed the 122-metre-cliff, Bear's Reach in California in four minutes and 25 seconds. That's a jaw-dropping 27 metres per minute. The average climber takes three hours on the route! Sadly, Dan's thrill-seeking nature led to his early death in a cliff-jumping accident in 1998.

Rising superstar

Born in 1990, Charlotte Durif was already the best female onsight sport climber by the time she was 15 – a phenomenal achievement. She was introduced to the mountains at an early age by her father, who took her with him on mountaineering trips. They camped on portaledges on rockwalls and icefields. She started climbing when she was nine.

Strongest climber?

John Gill is a US climber and boulderer who made an enormous contribution to climbing by bringing gymnastic training techniques to the sport. Many climbers train by performing pull-ups on a bar or fingerboard. Some are strong enough to pull themselves up by one arm. John Gill was the first person ever to pull himself up by just one finger.

chapter 6: legendary rock

El Capitan, Yosemite
National Park, USA

Some rock routes are as famous as the people who climb them. A boulder may look insignificant to most people, but may be known throughout the climbing community because it has an extremely hard problem on it.

The Nameless Tower

The Nameless Tower

Even small crags may boast internationally renowned routes that draw climbers from all over the globe. The fame of the rock is due to the difficulty of the climbing, and the beauty of the route. Rock that is both notoriously hard to climb and also breathtakingly beautiful is often the best-known of all.

One such rock is pictured here: The Nameless Tower, one of the Trango Group of rock spires which rise from the Baltoro Glacier in Pakistan's Karakoram Mountains.

This incredible vertical rock-tower, its summit at almost 6,250 metres, rises over a kilometre above the surrounding mountain ridge. It was first climbed in 1976 by Joe Brown, Mo Anthoine, Martin Boysen and Malcolm Howells.

**Todd Skinner climbs
The Nameless Tower**

**Todd Skinner at camp
in Pakistan, 1996**

In 1995 American Todd Skinner gathered together a team of elite climbers to free climb the entire east face of The Nameless Tower. They flew to Pakistan, where they bought the food and cooking fuel they would need. They had to hire 80 porters to carry it all.

They planned to take two weeks on the upper wall, but, in the end difficult climbing and stormy weather meant they spent two months up there. Sheer willpower and tenacity eventually got them to the top. Sadly, Todd Skinner died climbing on Leaning Tower (Yosemite Valley, USA) in 2006.

El Capitan dominates the entrance to Yosemite Valley. A towering rock face of sheer granite, it rises 1,100 metres above the green meadow floor. In 1957, American Warren Harding decided to climb it.

Another climber had recently made the first ascent of Half Dome, further down the valley. Harding knew that the only rock climbing achievement that could overshadow that would be the ascent of El Capitan. The project took him and his companions 18 months.

During this time they repeatedly climbed and descended the rock face; getting higher each time, drilling bolts, and attaching fixed ropes which they left in

El Capitan, Yosemite, USA

The Nose

Lynn Hill: "I still feel that the most important part of climbing is having fun with your friends."

Warren Harding reached
the top of The Nose in 1958

place over the winter. When they climbed again in the spring the ropes had weakened, and one snapped. Luckily the climber fell onto a ledge not far below. Finally Harding reached the top on November 12th 1958.

In 1993 Lynn Hill approached El Capitan with a dream in her heart. Although The Nose had been climbed several times since Harding's historic ascent, no one had successfully climbed it free. Lynn was a superbly strong and experienced climber who had won over 30 international climbing competitions. She free-climbed The Nose in four days — one of the greatest rock climbing achievements of all time. A year later, Lynn free-climbed the whole route in less than a day.

The North Face of the Eiger, or 'Ogre' – a mountain in the Swiss Alps – is one of the most notorious climbs in Europe. It 1,800 metres of vertical rock and ice, wracked by storms, rock falls and avalanches.

The North Face

The Ogre

In 1935, two brave young mountaineers arrived from Munich. They camped in a cowshed and studied the face through binoculars. They hoped to be the first to climb the North Face, or Nordwand.

Max Sedlmayer and Karl Mehringer battled up the North Face for five days. Ascending the wall involved both rock and ice climbing. The weather got worse and worse. They eventually died in bitter cold at a height of 3,298 metres.

A railway line runs up inside the Eiger (in the background); the railway tunnel has a window looking out from inside the rock face

In the years to follow, many climbers have attempted to scale the North Face, and some have been very successful. But of the failed ascents, the most tragic is probably that of Toni Kurz in 1936. He fought so valiantly to stay alive that his story is one of the saddest in mountaineering history.

In 1938, four men, Anderl Heckmair, Heinrich Harrer (both pictured above, 1978) Ludwig Vörg, and Fritz Kasparek successfully reached the top

Toni Kurtz was one of a party of four men who attempted to climb the Nordwand in 1936. At first all went well, but then the weather changed. Pouring rain froze to ice, covering the rock with a coating as hard and slippery as glass. Retreating in the appalling weather, the other three were all killed. Rescuers tried to reach Toni through the train tunnel window. Toni's left arm was frozen solid by frostbite, but he bravely climbed down towards his rescuers. A knot in his rope caught on his gear and he died of exhaustion and cold, just out of their reach. **59**

Some of the events that have shaped the history of rock climbing

Pierre Allain – one of the first climbers to love bouldering for its own sake

1935 French boulderer Pierre Allain invents the first rubber-soled climbing shoes. Before then, climbers wore nailed boots.

1945 Ex-military nylon ropes replace hemp ropes, making falling off safer. As a result, climbers attempt harder routes than ever before.

1952 Joe Brown climbs Cenotaph Corner, Wales, UK – one of the most inspirational early E grade or 'extreme' rock routes.

1958 Warren Harding aid climbs The Nose, El Capitan, Yosemite, USA. So many people come to watch there are huge traffic jams on the road below.

1961 John Gill solos the Thimble, South Dakota, USA – such a daring exploit that it remains the world's hardest climb for over 15 years.

1970s Sport climbing is born, in France. The bolts make climbing safer, and lead to a dramatic increase in technical standards.

1978 Ray Jardine patents Friends, the first sort of cam, which make crack climbing much safer as they can be fitted into awkward cracks.

1986 Johnny Dawes climbs Indian Face, Wales, UK – the first E9 trad route and so dangerous that it has only been climbed twice since.

1980s Crispin Waddy, Nick Buckley, Damian Cook and others invent and develop deep water soloing on the coast of Dorset, England.

Wolfgang Güllich – a great sport climber, he died in a car accident

1991 Wolfgang Güllich climbs Action Directe, Frankenjura, Germany – at 9a still one of the world's hardest sport routes.

1991 Catherine Destivelle opens a new route up the West Face of the Drus, France. The route can never be repeated: it collapsed in 1997!

1993 Lynn Hill free climbs The Nose, regarded by most climbers as the greatest ascent of all time. She proves that size doesn't matter: Lynn is only 155 cm tall.

2000 Chris Sharma climbs Mandala, V12, in Bishop, California, USA – a steep boulder problem that had been considered a great project for many years. His success fuels the worldwide passion for bouldering.

2002 Josune Bereziartu climbs Bain de Sang, 9a, Switzerland – the hardest route yet climbed by a woman, and within a hair's breadth of the top established male grade of 9a+.

Catherine Destivelle has excelled both on rock and in mountains

Glossary

Aid climbing Using a rope and gear to actually pull yourself up the rock, not just for protection in case of a fall.

Ascent A climb to the top.

Belay Device Rope brake used by the belayer to help them hold the climber if they fall.

Belayer Person holding the climber's rope, in case they fall.

Big wall A rock face too high for most climbers to get up in one day.

Bolts Permanent protection fixed into the rock face by drilling.

Bouldering Climbing fairly low down without a rope.

Boulderer A person who scales the lower section of rocks without a rope.

Cam A piece of climbing equipment that is placed in cracks of the rock face. The climber attaches their rope to it during a climb.

Crag A cliff or group of cliffs, in any location, which is or may be suitable for climbing.

Fixed ropes Ropes that are attached to the rock face and left in place to make retreat and later ascents easier. A technique sometimes used on very long, hard climbs, or when mountaineering.

Free climbing Climbing where a rope and gear are only used for protection in case the climber falls (also see 'aid climbing').

Gear The items the climber carries and uses as they climb to help protect them in case they fall. (Also sometimes used to mean all the stuff a climber uses, like boots, rope and chalk.)

Gear placement Crack or other place in the rock where protective gear may be slotted and to which the rope can be linked.

Gear ripping

Gear that has been placed pulling out when the climber falls.

Holding a fall/climber

Belaying a falling climber effectively, so that they do not hit the ground.

Leading

Climbing up the rock, from the bottom, clipping the rope to the protection (either temporary or permanent) in the rock as you go.

Pitch

Section of a long climb.

Problem

In bouldering, the route a climber takes in order to complete the climb.

Protection (permanent)

Bolts fixed into the rock, to which a climber can clip their rope.

Protection (temporary)

Bits of gear slotted into rock cracks (for example) to which the climber can clip their rope.

Quickdraw

Two metal ovals, each of which can be opened, that are joined together by special super-strong fabric tape. They are used to link the rope to the bolt or gear in the rock.

Rand

A rubber strip that runs around the bottom edge of a climbing shoe. It gives the shoe extra stability and more grip.

Route

The way the climber goes as they climb up.

Seconding

Following the leader up the rock face once they have reached the top (or top of the pitch), taking out any gear they placed as they led the route.

Sport climbing

Climbing using bolts for protection.

Trad climbing

Climbing where the rock face is left in its natural state and only temporary protection is placed.

Wire

A chunk of metal gear that a trad climber places in a crack to help protect them if they fall.

Index